graham and elaine   Jan 2016

To fellow travellers

through time
) hunting
                    ~~Peter~~

Memorials to the Mighty Eighth

January 2016

Duxford

After the American Air Museum
            re opens in March 2016

Hope you find this as an 'opener'
to the 8th

My favourites are

Maddingley — all yer round place
                for thought

Thorpe Abbots   100 BG   my
                    favourite — (with
                        cafe)

Grafton Underwood — Pioneer
                    BTT group and good
                new vial

Old Buckenham   Jimmy Stewarts old
                onit + flying club

good hunting   Peter S

To follow fro.
through time
good luck!
7

Memorials to the Mighty Eighth

Memorials, Plaques, Rolls of Honor, Museums
to the American 8th Air Force in World War Two

DENNIS F. LAIN

SERENDIPITY

First published in 2004 by
Serendipity
Suite530
37 Store Street
Bloomsbury
London

British Library Cataloguing-in-Publication data
A catalogue record for this book is available from the British Library

ISBN 1-84394-110-4

Printed and bound by Alden Group, Oxford

This book is written as a tribute to the 40,000 or so American Airmen
who gave their lives fighting from these bases in World War Two

Acknowledgements

I wish to thank all the friends and acquaintances - far too many to mention - that I have made whilst writing this book, for the many hours of answering questions, researching histories of bases, the roles they played in World War Two and advising me where to look for memorials. Thank you all.

How it all began,

It was Christmas 1944 when I first set foot on an American Air base when all the school children from villages in the area were invited to christmas parties at the local bases.We were collected in trucks and taken to the airfields where we had dinner played games and watched shows put on by the troops and returned to our homes tired but happy after a long day out. This was to remain a half forgotten memory for about 55 years until I visited my brother in 2000 when he asked if I had seen a photograph of me and some of my old school chums and some of our American friends in a book entitled *'OVER HERE'* that was taken that Christmas. This got me thinking that I had not been back to Seething Airfield since that day.

At the next opportunity my wife and I visited the old base and discovered that the Control Tower was now a museum to the 448th BG(H). On looking round the museum and taking photographs of the tower and memorials I thought a book should be published of the memorials to the very many men killed in the Second World War from the Mighty Eighth.

Having discovered that the last book published on this subject was about 10 years old and out of print and a large number of memorials have been erected since then, I began researching these memorials. I have travelled many miles photographing as many of the 8th USAAF. memorials as possible.

On these trips my wife and I have received a warm friendly welcome and many cups of tea from some of the most dedicated people I have ever met and who have been proud to show me flags, rolls of honor stained glass windows, books and other relics, not to mention much information. There are too many of these kind people to thank personally although as I have been told so often 'There arnt many un us left'. Where possible I have included a telephone number to contact museums and groups for anyone wishing for information, open days etc.

The aircraft , fighter and bomber groups and history of raids carried out by the Mighty Eighth have been well documented over the years as well as the bases themselves, thus I have included only a brief history of who built the airfields, who flew from them, missions flown and losses of various units, the uses of the airfields now and information on how to get to the memorials.

Also included are memorials from crash sites. This is ongoing and by no means complete as these are spread over most of the British Isles and quite a lot of Europe.

Dennis F. Lain.

CHRISTMAS 1944 SEETHING,

Officers left to right:
Lt. Carroll Michaels,(KIA.) Frank P. Law, Lt. Jack Potgeter.
W/O Jules Klingsburg, Lt. William Hammes.

Children left to right:
Norman Jermy (Died as a child), Dennis Lain (Author of this book),
Bob Littlewood, Jimmy Saunders and Ted Saunders.

Memorials to the Mighty Eighth.
Memorials Plaques, Museums Ect.
to the 8th USAAF.

Little Walden, Essex	5	102-104	165
Madingley, Cambridgeshire	7	105-108	
Martlesham Heath, Suffolk	2	109-110	369
Mendlesham, Suffolk	2	111-112	156
Metfield, Suffolk	1	113	366
Molesworth, Cambridgeshire	3	114-115	107
Mount Farm, Oxfordshire	3	116-117	234
North Pickenham, Norfolk	1	118	143
Nuthamstead, Hertfordshire	3	119-120	131
Old Buckenham, Norfolk	3	121-122	144
Oulton, Norfolk	1	123	
Podington, Bedfordahire	3	124-125	109
Polebrook, Northamptonshire	4	126-128	110
Rackheath, Norfolk	5	129-131	145
Rattlesden,Suffolk	3	132-133	126
Rayden, Suffolk	4	134-136	157
Ridgewell, Essex	2	137-138	167
Rougham, Suffolk	5	139-141	468
Seething, Norfolk	4	142-144	146
Shipdham, Norfolk	7	145-148	115
Snetterton Heath, Norfolk	4	149-151	138
Steeple Morden, Cambridgeshire	4	152-154	122
Sudbur,y Suffolk	4	155-157	174
Thorpe Abbots, Norfolk	7	158-161	139
Turleigh, Bedfordshire	3	162-163	111
Tibenham, Norfolk	1	164	124
Wattesham, Suffolk	3	165-166	377
Watton, Norfolk	5	167-169	376
Wendling, Norfolk	4	170-172	118
Westhampnett, Sussex	1	173	352
Wormingford, Essex	2	174-175	159

Memorials etc. near crash sites.

Ashby, Suffolk	1	176
Aston Clinton, Buckinghamshire	1	177
Barsham, Suffolk	1	178
Carlton Rode, Norfolk	1	179
Cawston, Norfolk	1	180
Cheshunt, Hertfordshire	1	181
Greenstead Green, Essex	1	182
Hardwick, Norfolk	1	183
East Harling, Norfolk	1	184
Hemel Hempstead, Hertfordshire	1	185
Kirby Bedon, Norfolk	1	186
Norwich, Norfolk	1	187
Penn, Buckinghamshire	2	188-189
Princes Risebough, Buckinghamshire	1	190
Reedham, Norfolk	1	191
Thorpe Abbots, Norfolk	1	192
Upper Sheringham, Norfolk	1	193

Alconbury Cambridgeshire
Station 102
1st Air Division

Built 1938 for RAF.
Operational 1939-1942 by RAF.
8th.USAAF September 1942 - June 1945.
93rd BG(H) 9/42-12/42 B24s.
92nd BG (H) 1/43-9/43 B17s.
482nd BG(H) B17s & B24s.Main Group.
Acted as Pathfinders for other groups June 1943 - February 1944.
Pioneered radar and other bombing devices for 8th USAAF.
1 DUC.11/1/44 all 1st. Air Div. units.
27/5/43 500lb Bomb exploded whilst loading bombs killing 16 Men destroying
4 B17s and damaging 11 others.
Only 8th USAAF BG{H} raised in UK.
Other units raised at Alconbury 36th & 406th BS to drop supplies and arms to
Resistance fighters in occupied territories, The Carpet Baggers, Station 547
Abbots Ripton, 2 SAD. Built 1943.
Operational 1/3/44 Personnel moving in from Little Staughton in Bedfordshire
Site now industrial and accommodation for personnel from Molesworth.
Site 4 miles north of Huntington. How to get there: Turn east off A1M at
Alconbury, follow signs to main gate, no entry to site.
Memorial Plaque on Police Building at Main Entrance O/S ref.142.810 755

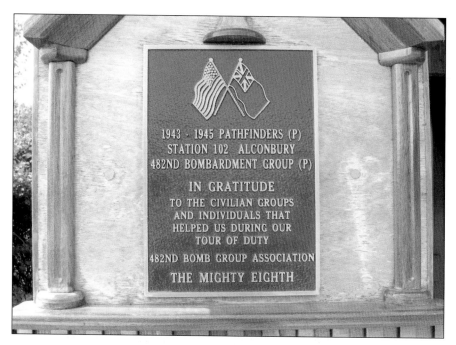

Inscription on Alconbury Plaque

Entrance to Alconbury Base

Andrews Field
Great Saling Essex
Station 485
3rd Air Division

Built 1942/43 by 817th US Engineer Battalion.

Operational May 1943 - October 1944.

96th BG {H} B17s May 1943 - June 1943 to Snetterton Heath

322nd BG {M} B26s. June 1943 - September 1944, To 9th. USAAF.October1943.

Base returned to RAF October 1944.

Only USAAF airfield to be named in honor of an American General,

Lt. General Frank M. Andrews killed in crash in Iceland.

Plaque Great Saling to Engineer Battalions.

Site now light aviation and farming.

Site 3 miles west of Braintree.

How to get there: Turn north off A120 between Gt. Dunmow and Braintree at Blakes End, signed Gt. Saling Memorial to 322 BG (M) on left in wooded area at old airfield access on left before Gt. Saling Village. O/S ref.167. 701 250.

Memorial to 817 Battalion US. Engineers on left in centre of Gt. Saling Village.

Main Memorial

13

Plaque on Main Memorial

Memorial to USAAF Engineering Battalions at Great Saling

Attlebridge Norfolk
Station 120
2nd Air Division

Built 1941 Richard Costain & Son Ltd.
Operational 1941/1942 by RAF.
8th USAAF October 1942 - July 1945.
319th BG(M) B26s October 1942 - November 1942.
RAF. March 1943 - February 1944.
466th BG (H) B24s March 1944 - July 1945.
Named, The Flying Deck.
Missions 232 losses Mia 47 plus 24 to other operational losses.
Plaque on Weston Longville village sign near church.
Plaque in church.
Stone memorial on Crossroads.
Control Tower part of offices for turkey farm.
Site now Turkey Farm and Agriculture.
How to get there: Turn north off A47 Honington Bypass signed Weston Longville.
Follow this road to Weston Longville Church, Roll of Honor in Church Plaque on
village sign. Return towards A47 take 2nd turn on left Weston Green road for
stone memorial O/S133 098145 on crossroads.

Stone Memorial

Village Sign and Memorial near Weston Longville Church

Flag and Roll of Honor in Weston Longville Church

Bassingbourn Cambridgeshire
Station121
1st Air Division

Built 1937/1938 John Laing & Son Ltd.

Extended 1942 W&C French Ltd.

Operational 8 USAAF .October 1942

91st BG (H) October1942 - September 1945. B17s.

94th BG (H) April 1943 - May 1943, B17s.

Missions 340 losses Mia. 197 highest in all 8th AF. Bomb Groups.

2 DUCs. 11/1/44 Oschersleben. 4/3/43 Hamm.

Name, Ragged Irregulars.

Tested first flak suits in 8 AF. March 1943.

11/4/44 General Eisenhower named B17 General Ike, using bottle of Mississippi water.

B17 Memphis Belle left from Bovingdon for USA after completing 25 missions 9/6/43.

B17 909 completed 140 missions without mechanical turn back.

1st. 8th.USAAF Unit. to complete 100 missions.

Museum in Control Tower, at least four plaques and memorial on site, plus memorial Stone in Royston Park.   How to get there: North from Royston on A1198. Memorials inside main gates of Army Barracks on left Memorial to 323 B. Sqn. on right side of A1198 opposite end of runway O/S ref.154 338 469.   Contact, 01359 221151.

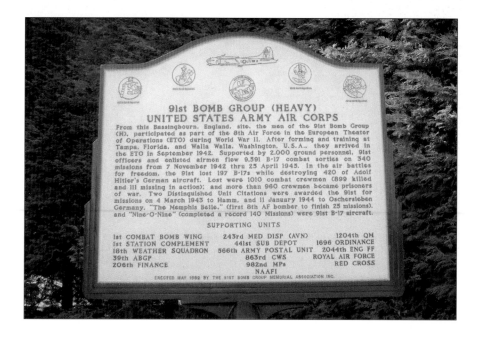

Part of Main Memorial, Bassingbourn

Memorial to 441 Sub. Depot, Bassingbourn

Part of Main Memorial, Bassingbourn

Memorial to 323 B. Sqd, Bassingbourn

Part of Main Memorial, Bassingbourn

Memorial to 91 BG(H) in Priory Gardens, Royston

Bassingbourn Control Tower

Inside Bassingbourn Tower

Bodney Norfolk
Station 141
1st Air Division

Built 1940.
Operational RAF. 1940/43.
8thUSAAF August 1943 - November 1945.
352nd FG P47s. July 1943 - April 1944, P51s. April 1944 - November 1945.
Missions 420 losses 118
Victories 520 Air plus 287 Ground.
Named The Blue Nosed Bastards of Bodney.
2 DUCs 8/3/44 Escort over Brunswick.
487 FS only 8th AF. Squadron to receive DUC for destruction of 23 enemy aircraft in one mission 1/1/45
Site now Army Training Camp and agriculture.
How to get there: Take B1108 from Watton to A1065, memorial on left outside Army Training Camp.
Entrance O/S. 144. 852 989.

Memorial outside Army Camp

Bottisham Cambridgeshire
Station 374
2nd Air Division

Built 1940 Operational 1941 / 1943 by RAF.
8th.USAAF. November 1943 - September 1944.
361st FG. P47s to May 1944 P51s. May 1944 onwards.
Missions 441 losses Mia. 81. victories 226 in air 105 plus on ground.
Memorial in Thomas Christian Way, named after group's first Commanding Officer.
Site now housing estate, agriculture and under A14 Trunk Road.
Site 6 miles East of Cambridge.
How to get there: North of A14 trunk road onto A1303. Memorial in village at Thomas Christian Way.
Also plaque in village church.

Memorial in Bottesham Church

Memorial in Thomas Christian Way

Bovingdon Hertfordshire
Station 112

Built 19411/42 John Laing & Son Ltd.

Operational July 1942 - September 1946.

11 Combat Crew replacement Centre July 1943 - September 1944. B17s.

92nd BG (H) 4 Missions 6/42-7/44. B17s.

US Transport Command 9/44-4/46.

US Air Transport Europe.

Air Technical Section testing 8th AF fighters.

Later home to 3rd Air Division,7581 Base Squadron and support units.

3 US Air Force 1949/1962.

Memorial plaque on wall of village hall to US. 3rd Airforce.

Site now custody centre, agriculture, industrial, and leisure complex.

How to get there, 2 miles South West of Hemel Hempstead on B4505 Chesham Road.

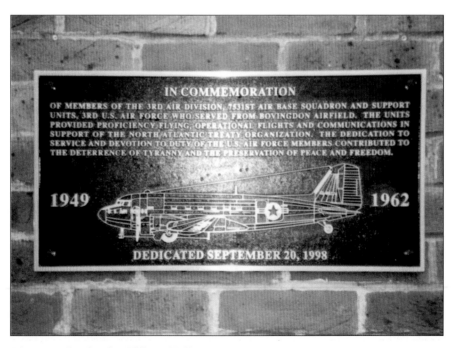

Plaque on Bovingdon Village Hall

Boxted Essex
Station 150
2nd Air Division

Built 1941/42 W & C French Ltd.
Operational 8th USAAF June 1943 - September 1945.
386 BG(M) B26s June 1943 - November 1943 transferred to 9th USAAF.
354th Fighter Group P51s November 1943 - April 1945.
Missions 55 losses Mia. 47 victories 169.
56th Fighter Group P 47s (The Wolf Pack)
Missions 447. victories air 647 ground 311.
2 DUCs 20/2/1944 destroying 98 enemy aircraft,
18/9/1944 Holland in support of airborne forces.
Destroyed more enemy aircraft than any other 8th USAAF Group.
First 8th USAAF group to fly P47, only group to fly P47s throughout war.
Site now fruit farm and agriculture.
Memorial at end of runway Langham Moor.
How to get there: Take A12 from Colchester, turn left about 2 miles north from
junction with A14 onto Park Road Langham Moor.
Memorial on left. O/S ref.168 018312.
Museum proposed. Contact tel. 01206 865275.

Memorial at Langham Moor

Plaque on Boxted Memorial

Bungay Suffolk
Station 125
2nd Air Division

Built 1942 Kirk & Kirk ltd.

Operational November 1943 - July 1945.

446th BG(H) B24s (Bungay Buckaroos).

Missions 273 losses Mia. 58 plus 28 to other operational causes.

Lead 8th USAAF 2nd A.D. on 1st Heavy Bomber Mission on D Day.

706th B/ Sqn. Flew 62 consecutive missions without loss.

(Ronnie)believed first B24 to reach 100 missions.

Site now chicken farm and agriculture.

How to get there: Memorial plus original Fountain Base from outside 2nd Air Division Library in Norwich. At Flixton in Norfolk & Suffolk Aviation Museum behind The Buck Public House on B1062 road. New Memorial erected on Airfield September 2003. Also small plaque on gate at Flixton Church and another in Bungay Community Centre in Upper Olland Street.

Contact tel. 01986 894169.

Memorial in Norfolk & Suffolk Aviation Museum

Plaque on Bungay Memorial in Flixton Museum

New Bungay Memorial erected 2003

Part of Fountain from outside 2nd Memorial Library in Norwich

Chalgrove Oxfordshire
Station 465

Built 1942 - 1943.

December 1944 to 9th USAAF.

30th Photo Reconnaissance Squadron. (P38s.)

February 1944 10th Photographic Group.

March 1945 7th Photographic Group moved from Mount Farm Oxfordshire till December 1945.

Site now Martin–Baker Industries.

How to get there: turn north off the B480 Stadhampton to Watlington road to Chalgrove Village. Memorial on left opposite John Hampton Memorial. O/S ref.164 646973.

Memorial outside Chalgrove Airfield

Cheddington Buckinghamshire
Station 113

Built 1941/1942 W &C French Ltd. Extended 1943.

Operational 8th. USAAF. September 1942 - September 1945.

44th BG(H) B24s September 1942 - November 1942 left for Station 115.

No. 12 Combat Crew Replacement Centre (B24s.) November 1942 - February 1944.

858th Night Leaflet Squadron June 1944 - March 1945.

803rd Radio Counter Measures Squadron March 1944 - August 1944 becoming 36th Radio Counter Measures Squadron August 1944 - February 1945.

495th Fighter Training Group January 1945 - March 1945.

Memorial at gate. Contact 01525 377631.

Site now light aviation, industrial and agriculture.

How to get there: Turn north west off B489 Aston Clinton to Ivinghoe Road in Marsworth towards Long Marsdon Memorial on right at old airfield entrance. O/S 165 914 152.

Memorial at main gate

Stone on Cheddington Memorial

Chelveston Northamptonshire
Station 105
1st Air Division

Built 1941/1942 Taylor Woodrow Ltd.
Operational December 1942 August 1945.
305 BG(H) B17s, named Can Do.
Missions 337 losses Mia.154,
2 DUCs 11/1/44 all 1st Air Division Groups, 4/4/43 Paris.
2 Medals of Honor, 1st Lt.William R. Lawley 20/2/44
1st Lt. Edward S. Michael 11/4/44.
442nd BS. pioneered first 8th USAAF night attacks.
Under Col. Lemay group pioneered formation and bombing procedures
that became standard practice for 8th USAAF.
Site now industrial and agriculture
Site 3 miles East of Higham Ferrers.
How to get there: South of A45 onto A6 at Higham Ferrers East, turn east onto
B645 for Chelveston turn right to Chelveston Church.
Memorial plaque on Church Tower. Memorial sign at gate and The Governors
Book inside church commemorating donations made to the church by the United
States to repair the church. O/S ref. 153 989 692.

Book of Governors in Chelveston Church

Memorial Plaque on wall of Chelveston Church

Sign outside Chelveston Church

Chipping Ongar Essex
Station 162

Built 1942 US Engineers.

387th BG (m) B26s.

September 1943 - October 1943.

Transferred to 9th USAAF. October 1943.

Site now agriculture.

387th BG(M) history in Blake Hall Airscene Museum near Bobbingworth, Contact tel.01277 841098.

How to get there: Signed on A414 at Bobbingworth O/S ref 167 539051.

Also Montage in Willingale Church O/S ref 167 597073.

Montage in Willingale Church

Blake Hall 387th BG(M) Museum

Debach Suffolk
Station 152
3rd Air Division

Built 1942/1943 US Engineer Battalions.

Operational April 1943 - August 1945.

493 BG(H) B24s/B17s, Named Heltons Hellcats.

Missions 158, losses Mia. 41 other operational causes 31.

B24s April 1944 - August 1944, 47 missions.

B17s. August 1944 - August 1945, 111 missions.

Last 8th USAAF group to become operational.

Col. Robert B. Landry only man to command both fighter and bomber groups in USAAF.

Site now industrial and agriculture.

How to get there: Turn south off B1078 Wickam Market to Needham Market Road, at Grove Farm Clopton, turn right into Snipe road.

Memorial set back on left in front of office building, O/S ref. 156 230 540.

Also Memorial in Clopton Church. Contact 01473 737293.

Debach Memorial

Part of Memorial

Flag and Roll of Honor in Clopton Church

Debden Essex
Station 356
2nd Air Division

Built for RAF. 1935/1937 W.C.French Ltd.
Operational 8th.USAAF September 1942 - July 1945.
4th Fighter Group named The Eagles,
Spitfires September 1942 - April 1943, P47s April 1943 - February 1944,
P51s February 1944 - July 1945.
Missions ? losses 241. victories air 538, ground 469
DUC. March /April 1944 destroying 123 enemy aircraft.
Formed from RAF Eagle Squadrons .
Highest number of enemy aircraft destroyed in 8th USAAF.
First 8th USAAF Fighter Group to fly over Germany 26/7/1943.
Site now Army Barracks.
How to get there: Turn west off B184 Gt. Dunmow to Saffron Walden Road
signed for Elder street and Carver Barracks.
Memorial inside main gate near Guardroom. OS ref. 154 570 345.

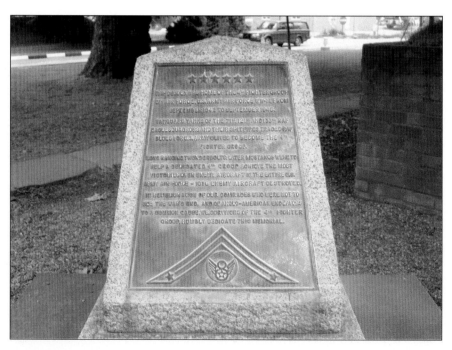

Debden Memorial

Deenethorpe Northamptonshire
Station 128
1st Air Division

Built 1943 John Laing & Son Ltd.
Operational October 1943 - June 1945.
491st BG(H). B17s.
Missions 255, losses Mia. 95.
2 DUCs 11/1/44 all 1st Air Division. 20/2/44 Leipzig.
2nd best bomb accuracy in 8th USAAF.
Site now light aviation and agriculture.
Site 9 miles north north East of Kettering.
How to get there: Memorial in lay by on north side of A427road, 3 miles east of
Weldon. O/S ref. 141 950 896. Also stained glass window in Weldon Church.

Stained glass window in Weldon Church

Roadside Memorial Deenethorpe

Deopham Green Norfolk
Station 142
3rd Air Division

Built 1943 John Laing & Son Ltd.
Operational January1944 - August 1945.
452 BG(H) B17s.
Missions 250 losses Mia 110 plus other losses 48.
DUC 7/4/45 Kaltenkirchen.
2 Medals of Honor 1/L.Donald J. Gott 9/11/44 ,
2/L.William E. Metzger,9/11/44.
Group had more COs than any other BG during hostilities.
Memorial on end of runway.
Plaques on Hingham Church wall and at Attleborough Railway Station
Site now agriculture.
How to get there: Turn south off B1108 road at Hingham Church,
memorial plaque at church gate, continue towards Gt. Ellingham for about
2 miles, turn left for Deopham Green Memorial on airfield
O/S ref. 144 028 988.
Also plaque on wall at Attleborough Railway Station.

Deopham Green memorial

Memorial at Hingham Church Gate

Memorial at Attleborough Railway Station

Duxford Cambridgeshire
Station 357
3rd Air Division

Built 1919.

Operational 8th USAAF April 1943 - October 1945.

78th FG. P38s. October 1942 February 1943 , P47s.February 1943 - December 1944. P51s December 1944 - 1945.

Missions 430 losses 167 victories 338 air plus 358 ground.

2 DUCs 16-23/9/44 support of airborne forces over Holland.

16/4/45 ground strafing Czechoslovakia.

1st. triple kill on one operation.

Only group to fly P38s P47s. and P51s.

1st strafing attack 30/7/43.

Shot down 1st ME 262 claimed by 8th USAAF.

Site now imperial War Museum plus US. Air Museum.

Memorial near old main gate.

Site 8 miles south of Cambridge.

How to get there: Turn off M11 at junction 10 onto A505 towards Royston, follow signs for Duxford Museum. O/S ref.154 456468.

Tel. No. 01223 835000.

Duxford Control Tower

American Air Museum Duxford

Memorial Screen of the Missing, Duxford

B17 Sally B at Duxford

Earls Colne Essex
Station 358
3rd Air Division

Built 1942.
Operational 8th. USAAF. May 1943 - October 1943.
94th.BG(H). B17s May 1943 June 1943 left for Rougham.
323rd. BG(M). B26s. June 1943 transferred to 9th Air Division October 1943.
Memorial in Marks Hall Gardens 4 miles S/E of Halstead.
How to get there. Turn North off Coggeshall bypass onto B1024,
turn left after about $\frac{1}{4}$ mile to Marks Hall Arboretum. Memorial in woods
$\frac{1}{4}$ mile from car park. O/S ref.168 843 264.

Memorial at Marks Hall

Plaques on Obelisk

East Wretham Nofolk
Station 133
1st Air Division

Built 1940. RAF. 1940 - 1943.

Operational 8th USAAF October 1943 - October 1945.

359th. Fighter Group,P47s October 1943 - May 1944.

P51s May 1944 - October 1945.

Missions 253, losses106 victories air 253 ground 98

DUC. 11/9/1944 Merseburg defence of bombers.

Site now Army Training Camp and agriculture. 6 miles N/E of Thetford.

How to get there: Turn left off A1975 Thetford to Watton Road at East Wretham.

Plaque on War Memorial outside Church O/S ref. 144 915 906.

War graves in churchyard, also Memorial plaque to359th FG. out side

Council Offices in Thetford near Thomas Paine Statue.

Memorial outside Council Offices in Thetford

Plaque on War Memorial at East Wretham Church

Eye Suffolk
Station 134
3rd. Air Division

Built 1942/1943 US Engineer Battalions.
Operational April 1944 - August 1945.
490 BG(H). B24s. April 19 August 1944
B17s August 1944   August 1945.
Missions 158 losses Mia. 22 plus 32 to other operational causes.
Lowest Mia. losses of any group in 8th USAAF. for extended period.
Site now industrial and agriculture.
Memorial in Brome Street.
How to get there: Turn east off Norwich to Ipswitch road, turn left after 150yds to
Brome Memorial on left in Brome Street, replica well cover with plaques.
O/S ref. 144 154 767.

Plaque on Eye Memorial

Plaque on Eye Memorial

EYE memorial at Brome Street

Fersfield Norfolk
Station 554
3rd Air Division

Built 1943 – 1944.

Operational July/1944 – January/1945.

US Navy Unit number 1 B24s. 2 Missions, ANVIL from Dunkeswell ,Devon.

388th BG(H) – 569th Sqn. Knettishall B17s. 17 Missions, APHRODITE.

Aphrodite plus Anvil projects whereby war weary B24s and B17s were stripped out loaded with 20000 lbs of explosive and flown by pilot and engineer who abandoned plane after take off it then being flown by radio control to target. Missions 19.

12/8/1944 B24 from number 1 US Navy unit blew up killing Lt Joseph Kennedy, brother of future President of The United States and his Flight Engineer.

Site now agriculture.

There is no memorial on site but numerous huts and buildings remain.

How to get there: take A1066 road from Thetford to Diss, turn north for Fersfield after South Lopham pass through Fersfield to Old Airfield.

O/s ref.144 072842.

Huts at Fersfield

Getting back to nature at Fersfield

Fowlmere Cambridgeshire
Station 378
3rd Air Division

Built 1940 modified1943 W&C French Ltd.
Operational 8th USAAF. May 1944 - October 1945.
389th Fighter Group P51s.
Missions 264, losses Mia.97 victories air 329 ground 440.
DUC.10-11/9/44 destruction of 58 enemy aircraft on escort missions.
Highest number of enemy aircraft destroyed in one year.
Tested Berger G suits for 8th USAAF.
Only group to claim over one hundred strafing victories on two occasions
105 4/4/45, 118 16/4/45.
Site now light aviation and agriculture.
How to get there: Turn north offA505 Royston to Duxford road onto B1368
to Fowlmere, turn left onto concrete road to Manor Farm, memorial set back from
road just before fsarm, O/S ref. 154 416 450.
Also small plaque on Chequers pub sign and at Village School.

Pub sign in Fowlmere

Fowlmere Memorial

Close up of Memorial

Framlingham Suffolk
Station 153
3rd Air Division

Built 1942/1943 Haymills Ltd.

Operational May 1943 - August 1945.

95th BG(H) May/June 1943 prior to moving to Horham.

390th BG(H) B17s. July 1943 - August 1945.

Missions 300, losses Mia. 144 plus 32 to other operational causes.

2 DUCs.17/8/1943 Regensburg all 4th Bomb wing groups 14/19/1943 Scheinfurt.

Hewitt Dunn only man to fly one hundred missions with 8th USAAF with 390 BG(H).

Control tower museum on site, site now agriculture.

How to get there: Turn north off A12 road 1½ miles north of Wickham Market, pass through Marlesford towards Gt.Glenham, follow signs for museum about 1½ miles from Marlsford . O/S ref. 156 387 607.

Contact 01376 320848.

Framlingham Museum and Memorials

Memorials at Framlingham

Glatton Cambridgeshire
Station 130
1st Air Division

Built 1943 US Engineers.
Operational January 1944 - July 1945.
457th BG (H) B17s.
Missions 237 losses Mia. 83.
Memorial in Connington churchyard.
Site now aviation and agriculture.
How to get there: From A1M at Junction 16 Normans Cross takeB1043 south alongside A1M to sign left for Connington, follow road towards Holme, Connington Church is on your right on leaving Connington.
O/s ref. 142 181 859.

Glatton Memorial

Rear of Glatton Memorial

Goxhill Lincolnshire
Station 345

Built 1940/1941 for RAF. John Laing & Son Ltd.

Operational 8th USAAF. August 1942 - march 1945.

August 1942 52nd Fighter Group Spitfires

October 1942 81st Fighter Group P38s /F400s.

December 19427 8th Fighter Group, P38s changing to P47s and moving to Duxford April 1943.

June 1943 353 Fighter Group P47s moving to Metfield August 1943.

August 1943 365 Fighter Group P45s moving to Martlesham Heath September 1943.

December 1943 496th Fighter Traing Group with 2 Squadrons, 554 Sqn operating P38s and 555th Sqn. Training crews for both 8th and 9th USAAFs.

496th Fighter Training Group moved to Halesworth December 1944.

Base returned to RAF. January 1945 .

Site now mainly agriculture.

How to get there: Take A15 road south of Humber Bridge at junction with A1077 turn east, pass through Barton on Humber and in Barrow on Humber take minor Roads to Goxhill, take Howe Lane and Horsegatefield road to airfield.

Contact 01469 532183.

Goxhill Memorial

Plaques on Goxhill Memorial

Plaques on Goxhill Memorial

Plaques on Goxhill Memorial

Grafton Underwood Northamptonshire
Station 106
1st Air Division

Built 1942/1943 George Wimpey Ltd.
Operational May 1943 - June 1945.
384th BG(H) B17s.
Missions 314, losses Mia. 159.
2 DUCs. 11/1/44 all 1st B D Group.24/4/44 Oberphafenhofen.
Claim to have dropped first and last bombs of World War 11 by 8th USAAF.
Site forms part of Duke of Bucleugh's Estate, 3 miles E/NE of Kettering.
How to get there: Turn north off A14 at A150 junction pass through
Crawford St. John and Crawford St. Andrew to Grafton Underwood,
Memorial stone on side of road at end of old runway, O/S ref.141 918 808.
Also stained glass window and plaque in church, key from Post Office.

Memorial at end of runway

Front and back of Grafton Memorial

Window and plaque in Grafton Underwood Church

Great Ashfield Suffolk
Station 155
3rd Air Division

Built 1942/1943 John Laing & Son Ltd.

Operational June 1943 - July 1945.

385 BG(H). B17s, named Vans Valiants.

Missions 296, losses Mia. 129 plus 40 from other operational causes.

2 DUCs 17/8/1943 Regensburg all 4 Bomb Wing Groups,12/5/1944 Zwickau.

Last group to be shot at 2/5/1945.

Site now mainly agriculture.

How to get there: Turn north off A14 eEast of Bury St. Edmonds signed for Ixworth at roundabout take road for Elmswell past railway station to Gt. Ashfield Church.

Memorial in churchyard also memorial altar and stained glass window in Church.

O/S ref. 155 982 624.

Contacts 01359 241045 and 01359 259283.

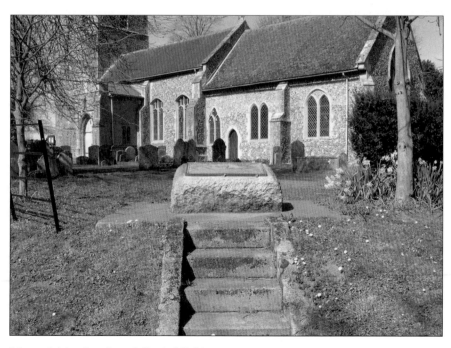

Memorial in churchyard Gt. Ashfield

Window in Great Ashfield Church

Altar in church

Memorial on altar

Memorial in churchyard. Great Ashfield

Great Dunmow Essex
Station 164

Built 1942/1943 US. Engineers.
386th BG(M) B26s.
June 1943 - October 1943.
Transferred to 9th USAAF. October 1943.
How to get there: Turn east off A11M at junction 8, take A120 towards
Gt. Dunmow memorial on left between Takely and Gt. Dunmow.
O/S ref. 167. 596 814.

Memorial beside A120 Road

Halesworth Suffolk
Station 365
2nd Air Division

Built 1942 John Laing & Son Ltd.
Operational July 1943 - June 1945.
56th Fighter Group P47s July 1943 - April 1944.
489 BG(H) B24s, May 1944 - November 1944 returned to United States.
Missions 106 losses Mia.29 plus 12 to other operational causes
489 BG(H) Museum at Hardwick Station 104.
5th Emergency Rescue Squadron, May 1944 - June 1945, flying specially
equipped P47s, Lifeboat carrying B17s and C10 Catalinas.
How to get there: take a144 Halesworth to Bungay road, turn right at Triple Plea
Roundabout follow Sparrow Hawk road to 56th Fighter Group Museum.
Memorials to all groups on right, O/S ref 156 401788 original fuel tank memorial
half mile past museum on left.
Contact 01986 872371

Original Drop tank Memorial at Halesworth.

56th Fighter Group Memorial

489th Bomb Group (H) Memorial

Memorial to 5th Emergency Rescue Squadron

Memorial and Roll of Honor in Holton Church to Halesworth Units

Halesworth Aviation Museum

Hardwick Norfolk
Station 104
2nd Air Division

Built 1941/1942 John Laing & Son Ltd.

Operational June 1942 - June 1945.

93rd BG(H) B24s named Teds Travelling Circus.

Missions 396 losses Mia.100 plus 40 to other operational causes.

2 DUCs 17/12/1942 operations in North Africa, 1/8/1943 Ploesti.

2 Medals of Honor Lt.Col. Addison E. Baker 1/8/1943,

Maj. John I. Jersted 1/8/1943.

Oldest B24 BG(H) in 8th USAAF.

Flew more missions than any other bomb group in 8th USAAF.

Most travelled group 8th USAAF.

B24 Boomerang first B24 to fly 50 missions.

Site now light aviation and agriculture.

How to get there: Turn west off B1332 Norwich to Bungay road south of Woodton, follow road through Topcroft Street, turn left at junction then right onto concrete road for Airfield Farm. O/S ref 134 264 904.

93rd BG Museum on site also 489th BG(H) Museum

Contacts 93rd BG. Museum 01508 531495. 489th BG(H) Museum 01986 874848.

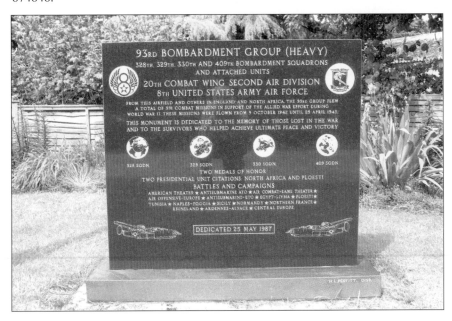

93rd BG(H) Memorial at Airfield Farm.

93rd and 489th Bomb Group (H) Museums at Hardwick

Hospitality Room at Hardwick

Plaque to 93rd BG (H) in Topcroft Church

Mural on wall at Hardwick

Harrington Northamptonshire
Station 179

Built 1943 US. Engineer Battalions.

Operational March 1944 - August 1945.

801st BG(H) including 36th and 406 B Sqns moving from Station 376 March 1944.

Redesignated 492 BG(H) "The Carpet Baggers" August 1944 parachuting agents, arms and supplies to Resistance Fighters in occupied territories, flying B24s B26s and later Mosquitoes.

Losses Mia. 28.

DUCs. 20/3/1945 to 25/4/1945 Germany and German occupied territories.

1958 - 1963 Thor missile site.

Site now agriculture.

5 miles west of Kettering.

How to get there: Turn South off A14 onto A508, go through Maidwell to Lamport, in about 3 miles memorial on right set back from road. Follow along this road towards Herrington, museums along track on left before crossing A14 bridge.

Memorial O/S ref. 141 778 778.

Harrington Memorial on end of runway

Back of Memorial showing crack

Sign for Harrington Museums.

Hethel Norfolk
Station 114
2nd Air Division

Built 1941/1942 W & C French Ltd.
Operational November 1943 - May 1945.
389 BG(H) B24s named "The Sky Scorpions".
Missions 321 losses 116 plus 37 to other operational causes.
DUC. 1/8/1943 Polesti.
Medal of Honor Lloyd H. Hughes 1/8/1943.
Site now home to Lotus Cars and agriculture.
How to get there: Turn south off A11 road at Wymondham, follow signs for Lotus Cars to main gate, pass on down lane to barrier, turn right through gate, follow track turning right beside wood to 389 BG. Chapel Museum. O/S ref.144 163 008.
Also memorial in Hethel churchyard and Roll of honor in church.
O/S/ref.144 171 004.
Contact 01593 697147.

Mural in Hethel Chapel Museum

Hethel Memorial in Church Yard

Roll of Honor in Hethal Church

Sign outside Hethel Chapel Museum

Model of Hethel Airfield

Honington Suffolk
Station 375
1st Air Division

Built 1935/1936 for RAF
Operational 8th USAAF February 1944 - November 1945.
364 Fighter Group P38s February 1944 - July 1944,
P51s July 1944 - November 1945.
Missions 342 losses 134 victories 256 air 193 ground.
DUC. 27/12/1944.Defence of bombers over Frankfurt.
Site now RAF. Regiment Base.
How to get there: Turn west off A1188 Thetford to Ixworth road at
Honington to Air Base entrance. Memorials at main gate O/S ref.144 469 783.
Also Station 595 Troston, No.1 SAD.

Memorial at Honington main gate

Memorial to 1st SAD. Honington

Memorial to 364th Fighter Group

Memorial at Honington to 1st Scouting Force

Horham Suffolk
Station119
3rd Air Division

Built 1942.
Operational May 1942 - August 1945.
47 BG(L) A20s. May 1942 - January 1943 left for 12th USAAF.
323 BG(M) B26s. January 1943 - June 1943 left for Earle Colne .
95th BG(H) June 1943 - August 1945.
Missions 320 losses Mia.157 plus 39 to other operational causes.
3 DUCs 17/8/43 Regensburg, 10/10/1943 Munster, 4/5/1944 Berlin.
Only 8th USAAF group awarded 3 DUCS.
Last aircraft lost by 8th USAAF went down in sea 7/5/45.
First 8th USAAF group to bomb Berlin 4/3/44.
Site now industrial and agriculture.
How to get there: From A140 take B1117 road west through Eye to
Horham Memorial at Horham Church O/S 156 210 724.
Also flag in Stradbrook church and Red Feather club in airfield.
Contact 01379 668458

Memorial at Horham Church

Memorial opposite Church at Horham

Horsham St. Faiths Norfolk
Station 123
2nd. Air Division

Built 1939 for RAF. Enlarged 1943
Operational September 1942 - December 1942 319th BG(M) B26s.
April 1943 - July 1943 56th FG. P47s.
January 1944 - July 1945. 458th BG(H). B24s.
Missions 240 losses Mia. 47 plus 18 to other operational causes.
14/3/45 1 B24 destroyed 7 more damaged when a gunner accidentally
fired his gun hitting the B24 next to him, no one was killed.
Carried out tests of Azon radio controlled bombs for 8th USAAF.
Site now Norwich International Airport..
City of Norwich Aviation museum on site. Contact 01603 893080.
2nd. Air Division Library in Norwich.
How to get there: Turn off A140 Norwich to Cromer road signed Airport
Terminal, plaques in Terminal Building. O/S 134 217 130.

Plaque to 458th BG (H) in Terminal Building

Plaque to 56th Fighter Group in Terminal Building at Horsham St Faiths

Kimbolton Cambridgeshire
Station 117
1st Air Division

Built 1941 W & C French Ltd.

Operational April 1942 - June 1945.

91 BG(H) B17s April 1942 - October 1942.

379 BG(H) B17s April 1943 - June 1945.

Missions 330 losses MIA141 plus 38 to other operational causes.

2 DUCs Operations 28/1/1943 - 31/7/44, all 1st A Division 11/1/44.

Flew more sorties and dropped more bombs than any other 8th USAAF group.

Pioneered 12 plane formation that became standard practice during 1944.

B17 Old Gappy flew 157 missions.

Site now agriculture and industrial.

How to get there: Turn west off A1 on B645 at St.Neots pass through Gt. Staughton and Kimbolton turn North onto B660 and in $\frac{1}{2}$ mile turn right for Stow Onga. Memorial in one mile outside Industrial Estate O/S 153 103 695. Also plaque in Kimbolton Church.

Kimbolton Memorial on airfield

Plaque in Kimbolton Church

Kings Cliff Northamptonshire
Station 367
1st Air Division

Built 1941 W & C French Ltd.
Operational 8th USAAF August 1943 - October 1945.
20th Fighter Group P38s August 1943 - July 1944.
P51s July 1944 - October 1945.
Missions 312 losses 132 victories 212 air 237 ground.
1 DUC. 8/4/44 sweep over Germany.
Best P51 maintenance record in later stages of war.
Site now agriculture.
How to get there: Turn west off A1 onto A47, pass through Wansford Village
towards Kings Cliff on unclassified road, memorial on right 1mile before
Kings Cliff Village O/S 141 022 892.

Kings Cliff Memorial

Knettishall Suffolk
Station 136
3rd Air Division

Built 1942/194W & C French Ltd.
Operational June 1943 - August 1945.
388th BG(H) B17s.
Missions 306 losses Mia. 142 plus 37 to other operational causes.
2 DUCs. 7/8/1943 Regensburg, 26/6/43 Hanover.
July 1943 560 Squadron moved to Fersfield for project Aphrodite to fly war
weary B17s filled with explosives by remote control.
Site now mainly agriculture.
How to get there: Turn south off A11 road onto B1111 to East Harling, on leaving
Village take minor road on left signed Gasthorpe pass over crossroads and
continue to junction signed Coney Weston, memorial on right.
O/S.ref. 144 469 783.

Knettishall Memorial

Part of Knettishall Memorial

Lavenham Suffolk
Station 137
3rd Air Division

Built 1943 John Laing & Son Ltd.
Operational April 1944 - October 1945.
487th BG(H) B24s. April 1944 - June 1944.
B17s. June 1944 - August 1945.
Missions 185 losses Mia. 48 plus 37 to other operational causes.
Led 3rd AD. In bombing Accuracy January 1945 till end of war.
Memorial plaque in Lavenham Market Place.
Plaques on Control Tower.
Airfield used in film '12 O'clock High'.
Site now agriculture.
How to get there: Take A134 Sudbury to Bury St. Edmunds road, turn east
in Alpheton, follow Lane to Control Tower, now offices, plaques on wall
of Control Tower O/S 155 896 529.

Memorial Plaque in Lavenham Market Place

Plaques on Lavenham Control Tower

Leiston Suffolk
Station 373
3rd Air Division

Built 1941/1942 John Mowlem Co.Ltd.

Operational October 1943 - August 1945.

358th Fighter Group P47s, November 1943 - February 1944 transferred to 9th USAAF.

Missions 17 losses 4.

357th Fighter Group P51s January 1944 - August 1945.

Missions 313 losses 128 victories 609 Air 196 ground.

2 DUCs 6/3/1944 Defence of bombers Berlin and Leipzig.

14/1/1945 action on Derben mission.

First P51 Group in 8th USAAF.

Fastest rate of victories in final year of war.

Site now agriculture.

How to get there, Turn east off A12 road at Yoxford onto B1122 Theberton, turn left opposite church then 2nd Left across old airfield, memorial on left near caravan park O/S ref.156 431638. Model P51 in caravan park and plaque on Old Post Office in Leiston.

Leiston Memorial o/s caravan park.

Plaque on Leiston Old Post Office

Leiston Memorial in caravan park.

Little Staughton Bedfordshire
Station 127
1st Air Division

Built 1942 for RAF.
Operational December 1942 - February 1944.
2 SAD. B17s.
1st Air Division.
Left for Abbots Ripon 1/3/44.
No 8th USAAF Memorial, Memorial to RAF Pathfinder Squadrons on site.
Site now light aviation, industrial and agriculture.
How to get there: East off B660 Bedford to Kimbolton road, follow signs to
Little Staughton, memorial about 2 miles south of village. O/S ref. 153 110613.

RAF. Path Finder Force Memorial

Little Walden Essex
Station 165
2nd Air Division

Built 1943.
Operational March 1944 - September 1945.
409 BG(L) A20s March 1944 - September 1944 to 9th USAAF.
361 Fighter Group P51s Moved from Bottisham September 1944 - February 1945.
Mission 441 losses 81 victories 226 air 105 ground.
493 BG(H) B24s February tTo March 1945 whilst runways at Debach were repaired.
Site now agriculture, Control Tower now private house, view by appointment only Tel. 01799 516365.
How to get there: Turn south off A1307 road in Linton onto B1052 towards Saffron Walden, Control Tower 2miles south of Hadstock O/S ref. 154 536 389
Also Anglo American Memorial Apse to 65 Fighter Wing USAAF at Bridge End Gardens, Saffron Walden.

Little Walden Control Tower

Plaques in Little Walden Tower

Anglo American Memorial Apse to 65th Fighter Wing in Saffron Walden

IN HONOURED MEMORY OF
THE OFFICERS AND MEN
OF THE 65TH FIGHTER WING OF THE
UNITED STATES ARMY AIR FORCE
AND THE MEN AND WOMEN OF THE
BOROUGH OF SAFFRON WALDEN
WHO GAVE THEIR LIVES IN
THE DEFENCE OF FREEDOM
1939-1945

Madingley, Cambridgeshire
American Military Cemetery
And Memorial

Cemetery established 1944 contains the graves of 3812 United States personnel killed in the 2nd World War.

The wall of the missing 144 metres long records 5125 personnel missing in action including Major Glen Miller and Lt. Joseph Kennedy, brother of President John Kennedy of the United States. The Memorial Chapel has a beautiful mosaic ceiling and a large map on which are recalled the huge efforts and operations carried out by the United States by land sea and air over Europe .

A Memorial Service is held here each year and a visit here is a very moving experience.

How to get there: Going north on the M11 turn west onto A1301, or from Cambridge head west on A1301, signed for American Memorial Cemetery.

O/S ref. 154 405596 Tel. 01954 210350.

Memorial Chapel at Madingley

The Wall of the Missing Madingley

Marlesham Heath Suffolk
Station 369
1st Air Division

Built 1917 for RAF.

Operational 8th USAAF November 1943 - November 1945.

356th Fighter Group P47s November 19 November 1944.

P51s November 1944 - November 1945.

Missions 413 losses 122 victories 201 air 75 ground.

DUC 17th to 23/9/44 Support to airborne forces in Holland.

Site now industrial and housing.

How to get there: North on A12 road east of Ipswich, turn right at roundabout past high towering building, turn right into Parade Ground Road, memorial on right O/S. ref 169 248 450. Also Control Tower Museum at Parkers Place off Eagle Way O/S ref. 169 240 456, Contact 01473 624510.

Martlesham Heath 8th USAAF memorial

Martlesham Heath Control Tower Museum

Complete Memorial Martlesham Heath

Mendlesham Suffolk
Station 156
3rd Air Division

Built 1943 for RAF.

Operational 8th USAAF. April 1944 - September 1945.

34th BG(H) B24s.April 1944 - September 1944.

B17s, September 1944 - September 1945.

Missions 170 losses Mia. 34 plus 39 to other operational causes.

Oldest Bomb Group to serve 8TH USAAF.

Only aircraft lost to enemy fighters, four over own base 7/6/1944.

Site now industrial and agriculture.

1000 ft. radio tower on site now used by emergency services.

How to get there: Memorial set back on east side of A140 Ipswich to Norwich road, north of Stonham Aspal, O/S ref. 155 120 634.

Mendlesham Memorial

Mendlesham Memorial

Metfield Suffolk
Station 366
2nd Air Division

Built 1942/1943 John Laing & Son Ltd.
Operational   August 1943 - April 1944 353rd FG. P47s.
April 1944 - August 1944. 491st BG(H) named The Ring Masters. B24s.
Missions 187
Losses Mia. 47 plus 23 to other operational causes.
August 1944 - June 1945 European division of Air Transport USSTAF.
15/7/44 Bomb dump exploded killing at least 5 men, writing off 5 B24s.
with 6 badly damaged plus several buildings.
Crater filled in late sixties.
Memorial on site.
Site now agricultural land.
How to get there: Take B1123 Harleston to Halesworth road, memorial set back
from road on left side 1^1/$_4$ miles from Metfield. O/S ref. 156 308 789.

Metfield Memorial

Molesworth Cambridgeshire
Station 107
1st Air Division

Built 1940 for RAF.
Operational 8th USAAF October 1942 - June 1945.
303 BG(H) B17s named Hells Angels.
Missions 364 Losses 165,
DUC. 11/1/1944 All 1st AD. Bomb Groups.
2 Medals of Honor Lt. Jack W. Mathis 18/3/1943
T/sgt. Forrest L.Vosier, 20/12/1943.
Knockout Dropper first B17 to complete 50 and 75 missions.
First 8th USAAF group to complete 300 missions.
Flew more missions than any other B17 group.
Now Military Intelligence collecting centre.
How to get there: Turn north off A14 road signed Old Weston, turn left in 100
yards to Brington Church, memorial plaques in church, continue north to airfield
gate on left, memorial inside gate. O/S ref. 142 088 770.

Molesworth Memorial

Back of Molesworth Memorial

IN MEMORY OF MEMBERS OF THE 303RD BOMBARDMENT GROUP (H) AND ITS ASSIGNED SUPPORT UNITS, STATIONED AT MOLESWORTH, WHO GAVE THEIR LIVES IN THE PERFORMANCE OF THEIR DUTIES IN THE DEFENSE OF THE FREE WORLD DURING THE PERIOD OF 12 SEPTEMBER 1942 - 11 JUNE 1945 DEDICATED BY 303RD BOMB GROUP ASSOCIATION JUNE 1984

Molesworth Memorial Plaque in Brington Church

Mount Farm Oxfordshire
Station 234

Built 1941 for RAF.

Operational 8th USAAF. July 1943 - May 1945.

7th PG. Flying P4-5-6s. Spitfire X1s and P51s.

DUC. 31/5/44 - 30/6/44 Photo coverage of Normandy Landings.

7th PG. Group moved to Station 465 Chalgrove Oxfordshire March 1945.

Memorials in village and in grounds of Dorchester Abbey.

Site now agriculture and quarries.

How to get there: Take A4074 Oxford to Henley on Thames road at Burcot Roundabout, at junction with A415 turn left into housing estate, memorial on right. O/S 164 572 961.

Mount Farm Memorial

Inscription on Mount Farm Memorial

Memorial Stone in Dorchester Abbey Gardens

North Pickenham Norfolk
Station 143
2nd Air Division

Built 1943/1944.

Operational 8th USAAF May 1944 - August 1945.

492 BG(H) B24s. May 1944 - August 1944.

Missions 64 Losses Mia. 51 plus 6 to other operational causes.

Highest loss rate for any B24 group in 8th USAAF over three month period.

Disbanded August 1944.

491 BG(H) B24s. August 1944 - July 1945. "The Ring Masters".

Missions 187 Losses 47 plus 23 to other operational causes.

DUC. 26/11/1944 Misburg .

Highest rate of operations of all B24 groups.

Missile base late 1950s/early 1960s.

Site now agriculture.

How to get there: From Swafham take B1077 South towards south Pickenham, take second road on left towards North Pickenham, memorial on left at start of village. O/S/ref.144 861 067.

North Pickenham Memorial

Nuthamstead Hertfordshire
Station 131
1st. Air Division

Built 1942 - 1943 US. Engineer Battalions.
Operational September 1943 - June 1945.
55th FG. P38s September 1943 - April 1944.
398th BG(H) B17s. April 1944 - June 1945.
Missions 195 losses 58.
Radio beacon on site memorial o/s Woodman public house in village.
Site now agriculture industrial and leisure.
How to get there: Turn east off A10 at Buckland for Barkway, at junction with
B1368, turn left then right for Nuthamstead, turn left in village
for Woodman Public House and memorial. O/S ref. 154 412 345.
Also stained glass window in Anstey Village Church.

Memorial outside Woodman Public House

Back of Nuthamstead Memorial.

Window in Anstey Church.

Old Buckenham Norfolk
Station 144
2nd Air Division

Built 1942/143 Taylor Woodrow Ltd.
Operational December 1943 - May 1945.
453 BG(H). B24s.
Missions 259 losses 58 plus 25 from other operational causes.
735 B Sqn. Completed 82 consecutive missions without loss.
How to get there: Take B1077 road from Attleborough to Old Buckenham, turn
left in village to village hall which includes the Memorial Hall subscribed
too by members of 453 BG(H) and contains memorabilia and Roll of Honor.
For airfield memorial follow road for about 1 mile, Flying Club Entrance on left
memorial outside Flying Club Offices O/S/ref. 144 073 932.
Contact 01953 483396.

Old Buckenham Airfield Memorial

Memorabilia in Memorial Hall at Old Buckenham

Roll of Honor in Old Buckenham Memorial Hall

Oulton Norfolk
Station ?

Built 1940 for RAF.
Used by 8th USAAF May 1944 - August 1944
803rd Radio Counter Measures squadron Lodger Unit.
Memorial near crossroads in village.
How to get there: Turn north east off Norwich to Holt road to Oulton,
pass over airfield and through Oulton Street to memorial.
O/S ref. 133 153 278.

Combined Memorial at Oulton

Podington Bedfordshire
Station 109
1st Air Division

Built 1941 for RAF. Extended 1942.

Operational 8th USAAF August 1942 - June 1943.

301st BG(H) B17s. August 1942 - November 1942 transferred to 12th USAA

92nd BG(H) B17s "Fame's Favoured Few" September 1942 - June 1945.

Missions 308 losses 154.

DUC 11/1/44 All 1st Ad Groups.

Medal of Honor F/O John C. Morgan 26/7/43.

Oldest Bomb Group in *th USAAF.

327 Sqn. Only 8th USAAF unit equipped with YB 40s for combat.

First BG to fly non-stop across Atlantic August 1942.

Flew Disney Rocket Bomb experimental missions early1945.

Site now drag racing strip, industrial, agriculture, Control Tower, private house.

How to get there: Turn west off A6 road 1 mile south of Rushton at Wymington to Podington Church, organ memorial to 92 BG(H).

Also new memorial on right of airfield road, O/S ref. 153 940 616.

New Memorial at Podington

Podington Church Organ repaired by 92nd BG(H)

Inscription on organ: When this organ is played we shall be remembered

Polebrook Northamptonshire
Station 110
1st Air Division

Built 1940/1941 for RAF extended 1942.
Operational 8th USAAF June 1942 - July 1945.
97th BG(H) B17s June 1942 - November 1942 transferred to 12th USAAF.
351st BG(H) B17s April 1943 - July 1945.
Missions 311 losses 134.
2 DUCs. 9/10/43 Anklam, 11/1/44 all1st AD .Groups.
Thor Missile site 1950s/1960s.
Site now agriculture.
How to get there: Turn south east from A605 road at Oundle onto minor road to
Polebrook, Memorial Chapel in Polebrook Church, pass through Polebook
towards Lutton, turn right at crossroads for Hemington Memorial on right,
O/S/ref. 142 100 878.

Polebrook Memorial

Polebrook Memorial

Chapel in Polebrook Church

Plaque commemorating the Posthumous Award of Medals of Honor to 1st Lt. Walter E. Truemper Navigator, and S/Sgt. Archibald Mathis Ball Gunner, killed when their B17 (Ten Horsepower) crashed returning from a raid over Germany. In Polebrook Church

Rackheath Norfolk
Station 145
2nd Air Division

Built 1943 John Laing & Son Ltd.
Operational 8th USAAF May 1944 - July 1945.
467th BG(H) B24s "Rackheath Aggies".
Missions 212 losses Mia 29 plus 19 to other operational causes.
Best overall bomb accuracy in 8th USAAF.
Col. Shower was only CO to bring BG to UK. and remain throughout hostilities.
B24 "The Witch" suffered over 300 flak holes and completed 130 missions.
29/12/44 2 B24s crashed on takeoff killing 15 crewmen.
Site now industrial and agriculture.
How to get there: Take A1151 Norwich to Wroxham road turn right at sign for
Rackheath Industrial Estate, turn left into Wendover road and follow to memorial.
O/S ref. 134 282 140
More Plaques outside Church in New Rackheath.
O/S ref.134 285 126.

Airfield Memorial at Rackheath

Close up of Rackheath Memorial and Plaque on New Rackheath Church Gate

Plaques outside New Rackheath Church

Rattlesden Suffolk
Station 126
3rd Air Division

Built 1942 George Wimpey Co. Ltd.
Operational May 1943 - August 1945
322nd BG(M) B26s May 1943 - October 1943 transferred to 9th. USAAF.
447th BG(H) B17s November 1943 - August 1945.
Missions 257 losses Mia. 97 plus 43 to other operational causes.
Medal of Honor 2/Lt. Robert E. Femoyer 2/11/44.
B17" Milk Wagon" set record for 3rd Div. with 129 missions and no turnbacks.
Memorial on side of road at High Town Green.
Site now gliding club and agriculture.
How to get there: Take second road south off Rattlesden to Felsham Road,
memorial on left in about 1¹/₂ miles O/S 155 972 571.
Also plaques etc. in control tower at Glider Club. Contact 01449 736687.

Roll of Honor in Control Tower Glider Club House

Rattlesden Memorial

Plaque on Control Tower at Rattlesden

Raydon Suffolk
Station 157
3rd Air Division

Built 1942 - 1943 US. Engineers.

Operational November 1943 - October 1945.

357th FG. P51s November 1943 - January 1944.

353rd FG. April 1944 - October 1945.

P47s April 1944 - October 1944 P51s October 1944 - October 1945.

Missions 447 losses 137.

Victories 330 air plus 414 ground.

DUC. Support of airborne landings in Holland 17-23/9/44.

Site now agriculture.

How to get there: East of Hadleigh to Raydon Road B1070, at entrance to Raydon take first turn on right, memorial on Right O/S155 061 397.

Also carved door and roll of honor in village church, key from cottage opposite church.

Raydon Memorial

Close up of Raydon Memorial

Door Memorial in Raydon Church

Book of Remembrance in Raydon Church

Ridgewell Essex
Station 167
1st Air Division

Built 1941 - 1942 for RAF.
Operational 8thUSAAF June 1943 - June 1945.
381st BG(H) B17s.
Missions 296 losses 131.
2 DUCs. 8/10/43 Bremen, 11/1/43 all 1st.Div. groups.
23/6/43 B17 blew up damaging others, 22 airmen and 1 civilian killed.
Memorial on site.
Museum in old hospital building.
Site now agriculture.
How to get there: North side of A604 Halstead to Haverhill road at top
of Oaken Hill at north end of Great Yeldham Village O/S 155 747 397.
Museum on site, Contact 01787 277 310.

Ridgewell Memorial

Old Hospital Buildings at Ridgewell now Museum

Roughham Suffolk
Station 468
3rd Air Division

Built 1942 Richard Costain Ltd
Operational December 1942 - December 1945.
332nd BG(M) 12/1042-6/1943 B26s.transfered to 9th USAAF .
94th BG(H) 6/1943 - 12/1945, B17s
Missions 325 losses Mia.153 plus other operational losses 27.
2 DUC 17/8/43 All 4th. BW units 11/1/44 Brunswick.
Glen Miller Concert 16/9/44.
Museum in Control Tower.
Memorial in Abbey Gardens Bury St. Edmonds.
Flying Fortress Pub near airfield.
Site now light aviation, industrial estate and agriculture.
How to get there: North off A14 about 2 miles east of Bury St. Edmunds
turn left through industrial estate to Control Tower Museum.
O/S 155 982 642. Contact 01359 271 471. Memorials in Rose Garden in grounds
of Bury St. Edmunds Abbey.

Rougham Control Tower Museum

Rougham Memorial and Plaque in Bury St.Edmonds Abbey Gardens

Seat made from B17 wing in Abbey gardens

Inscription on seat

Seething Norfolk
Station146
2nd Air Division

Built 1942/1943 John Laing & Son Ltd.
Operational 8th USAAF. October 1943 - July 1945.
448th BG(H). B24s.
Missions 262 losses Mia. 101 plus 34 to other operational causes.
22/4/1944 3 B24s shot down over airfield by night fighters.
Site now light aviation and agriculture.
How to get there: Turn east off B1332 Norwich to Bungay road between
Kirstead and Woodton into Harveys Lane, pass over crossroads to Toad Lane,
Control Tower Museum on left memorial near tower O/S ref. 134 318 955.
Also memorial outside Waveney Flying Club Offices, O/S/ref 134 319 960.
Plus memorial stone in Seething Church Yard O/S ref.134 318 455.
Museum Contact 01508 550 787.

Memorial outside Flying Club Offices at Seething

Seething Memorial near Control Tower

Memorial in Seething Church Yard

Seething Control Tower Museum.

Shipdham Norfolk
Station 115
2nd Air Division

Built 1941/1942.
Operational 8th USAAF. October 1942 - June 1945.
44th BG(H) B24s "The Flying Eight Balls".
Missions 343 losses Mia. 153 plus 39 to other operational causes.
2 DUCs. 14/5/1943 Kiel, 1/8/1943 Ploesti.
Medal of Honor Col. Leon W. Johnson 1/8/1943.
First group to be equipped with B24s.
Operated in UK. longer than any other B24 group.
First group to be awarded DUC. 14/5 1943.
Site now light aviation and agriculture and industrial.
How to get there: Turn off B1075 road in Shipdham signed Airfield Road, turn
left onto airfield, follow concrete road past farm to Flying Club Memorial plaque
and Memorabilia at Flying Club O/S/ref.144 981 080. Club Tel. 01362 820709
Memorial stone in churchyard O/S ref. 144958 074.
Also plaque on wall of Control Tower in Crane Hire Yard O/S ref. 144 990 070.

Shipdham Memorial plaque outside Flying Club

Shipdham Memorials in Church Yard and on Old Control Tower.

Shipdham Flying Club and Museum

Shipdham Museum.

Snetterton Heath Norfolk
Station 138
3rd Air Division

Built 1942/ 1943 Taylor Woodrow Ltd.
Operational June 1943 - November 1945.
386th BG(m) B26s. July 1943 - October 1943 transferred to 9th USAAF.
96th BG(H) B17s. June 1943 - November 1945.
Missions 321 losses Mia. 189 plus 50 to other operational causes.
2 DUCs 17/8/43 Regensburg, 9/4/44 Poznan.
Second highest losses in 8th USAAF highest 3rd BD.
First double strength bomb group in 8th USAAF.
Memorial Chapel in Quidenham Church.
New memorial on site at entrance to racetrack.
Museum at Eccles School.
Site now racetrack, industry, Sunday market and agriculture.
How to get there: Turn south off A11 road at Snetterton for entrance to Motor
Racing Circuit and Sunday Market.
Memorial at entrance to Racing Circuit O/S 144 008 905.
Also Memorial Chapel in Quidenham Church O/S144 029 877.
Contact 01379 634 762.

New Memorial at Snetterton Heath

Window in Memorial Chapel in Quidenham Church

Plaque in Quidenham Church

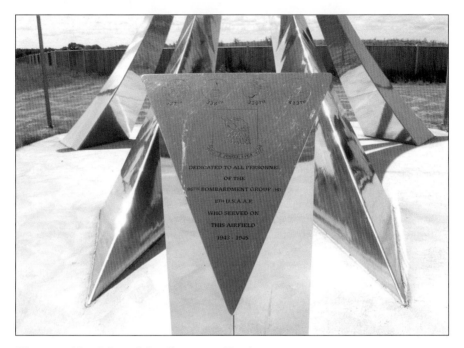

Plaque on New Memorial at Snetterton Heath.

Steeple Morden Cambridgeshire
Station122
2nd Air Division

Built 1941 for RAF. John Laing & Son Ltd.
Operational 8th USAAF, July 1943 - July 1945.
355th Fighter Group P47s July 1943 - March 1944
P51s March 1944 - July 1945.
Missions ? losses 175 victories 365 air 520 ground.
DUC 5/4/44 attacks on German airfields.
Destroyed more enemy aircraft by strafing than any other group.
Experimental Scouting Force later 2nd Scouting force stationed on site
1944 -1945.
Site now agriculture.
How to get there: Turn north off A505 Baldock to Royston road signed
Litlington, continue through village turning left at church, memorials on
left in 1 mile O/S ref. 153 230 424.
Also stained glass window in Litlington Church.

Steeple Morden Extended Memorial

Plaques on Gateposts at Steeple Morden

Stained glass window in Litlington Church

Sudbury, Suffolk
Station 174
3rd Air Division

Built 1943.
Operational March 1944 - August 1945.
486th BG(H) B24s March 1944 - July 1944,
B17s July1944 - August 1945.
Missions 188. losses Mia. 33 plus 24 to other operational causes.
834th Sqn. lost no aircraft or personnel on first 78 missions.
Memorial at gate and o/s St. Bartholomews Church.
Plaque on Town Hall.
Site now agriculture and industrial.
How to get there: Take B1115 Sudbury to Lavenham road, about 1 mile north of
Sudbury, memorial on right at airfield entrance.

Sudbury Memorial

Close up of Sudbury Memorial

Plaque on Sudbury Town Hall

Memorial outside St Bartholomews Church Sudbury

Thorpe Abbotts Norfolk
Station 139
3rd Air Division

Built 1942 John Laing & Son Ltd.
Operational June 1944 - December 1945.
100th BG(H) B17s named The Bloody Hundredth.
Missions 306 losses Mia. 177 plus 52 to other operational causes.
2 DUCs 17/8/43 Regensburg. 4-6-8/3/44 Berlin.
Large losses of aircraft at intervals throughout period of combat.
Control Tower Museum and Memorial on site.
Site now agriculture.
How to get there: Turn east off A140 road onto A143 towards Harleston,
turn north and follow signs for 100th BG museum in Control Tower.
O/S 156 188 813. Contact 01379 740708.

Plaques on Control Tower

Screen Head and Plaques in Thorpe Abbots Church

Thorpe Abbotts Museum

Inside museum

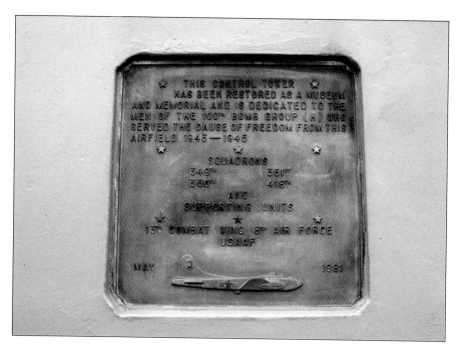

Plaques on Thorpe Abbotts Tower

Thurleigh Bedfordshire
Station 111
1st Air Division

Built 1941 W & C French Ltd. extended 1942/1943.
Operational 8th USAAF. September 19442 - 1945.
306 BG(H) B17s. "THE REICH WRECKERS".
Missions 342 losses 171.
2 DUCs 11/1/44 all First AD groups. 22/3/44 Bernburg.
Medal of Honor Sgt. Maynard H. Smith 1/5/43.
First man in 8th USAAF to complete a tour of duty T/sgt. M. Roscovich 5/4/43.
Princess Elizabeth named B17 "Rose of York" at Thurleigh.
Site now autodrome and industrial.
How to get there: North on A6 Bedford to Rushden road, turn right at Sharnbrook roundabout follow signs for airfield on left. Museum on airfield O/S ref. 153 039 608
Contact Tel. 01234 708715.
Memorial at Kelsoe road Thurleigh,
O/S ref.153 058 591.

Inscription on Thurleigh Memorial.

Thurleigh Memorial

Thurleigh Airfield Museum

Tibenham Norfolk
Station 124
2nd Air Division

Built 1942 W& C French Co. Ltd.
Operational November 1943 - May 1945.
445th BG(H) B24s.
Missions 282 losses Mia 108 plus 25 to other operational causes.
DUC 24/2/44 Gotha.
Highest group loss in single mission 30.
November 1943 film star James Stewart CO. 703th Sqn.
Site now glider club and agriculture.
How to get there: Turn West off A140 Norwich to Ipswich road, onto B1134
towards Attleborough, after passing Level Crossing take 2nd road left for
Smeath Common, turn left onto airfield, memorial outside Glider Club.
O/S/ ref. 144 148 890.

Memorial out side Glider Club

Wattisham Suffolk
Station 377
2nd Air Division

Built 1938 for RAF. John Laing & Son Ltd.
Operational 8th USAAF May 1944 - November 1945.
479th Fighter Group "Riddles Raiders".
P38s May 1944 - August 1944, P51s August 1944 - November 1945.
Missions 351 losses 69 victories 155 air 279 ground.
DUC. 18/8/1944 to 26/9/44 strafing airfields and air combat near Munster.
Last Fighter Group to join 8th USAAF.
First combat with enemy Jet aircraft 29/7/1944.
Site now Army Corp Base.
How to get there: West on B1178 road from Needham Market to Bilston, turn
right signed for Great Bricett and RAF Wattisham, gate one. O/S ref.155 023 513.
Plaque in museum inside base, open on Sundays 2.00 pm to 4.30 pm.
Contact 01449 678189.

Plaque in Wattisham Museum

Wattisham Museum

Nose Art in Wattisham Museum

Watton Norfolk
Station 376

Built 1939 for RAF John Laing & Son Ltd.

Operational 8th USAAF. January 1944 - July1945.

25th BG Reconnaissance 22/4/44 - 23/7/1945.

B24s April1944 - October 1944, Mosquito XV1s, October 1944 - July 1945.

36th and 406th Sqns. Later to become the reformed 492nd BG(H) moving in from Alconbury January to April 1944.

Site now awaiting development.

How to get there: Turn left off B1108 Norwich to Watton road into Portal Way, memorial to 25th BG(R) at top of Portal Way O/S/ref. 144 945 006.

Also Station 505 Neaton, No. 3 SAD B24 Depot.

Memorial to No 3 SAD in Griston churchyard with plaque and flag inside church.

Watton 25th BG(R) Memorial

Overall picture of Watton Memorial

Plaque to No.3 SAD in Griston Church

Memorial to 3rd SAD in Griston Churchyard

Flag in Griston Church

Wendling Norfolk
Station 118
2nd Air Division

Built 1942 Taylor Woodrow Ltd.
Operational August 1943 - June 1945.
392nd BG(H) B24s.
Missions 285 losses Mia.127 plus 57 to other operational causes.
DUC 24 /2/44 Gotha.
First B24 group in 8th USAAF .
Memorial at Beeston.
Site now industrial estate and agriculture.
How to get there: Turn north off A47 Dereham to Swafham road signed Beeston and Cranes Corner, memorial on right before Beeston Village O/S 132 913 150.

Wendling Memorial

Plaques on of Plinth Wendling Memorial

Plaque on plinth Wendling Memorial

Westhampnett Sussex
Station 352

Built 1940 for RAF.
July 1942 - October 1942 8th.USAAF.
31st Fighter group 8th USAAF.
Transferred to 12th USAAF October 1942.
First Group to operate with 8th USAAF.
Memorial on Goodwood Raceway.
Contact 01903 724967.

Westhampnett Memorial

Wormingford Essex
Station 159
3rd Air Division

Built 1943 Richard Costain Ltd.
Operational April 1944 - July 1945.
55th FG P38s. April 1944 - July 1944.
P51s. July 1944 - July 1945.
Missions ? losses 181 victories 316 air plus 268 ground.
2 DUC 3-13 /9/44 destruction 106 enemy aircraft on one mission.
19 /2 / 1945 Ground strafing achievements.
First P38 group in combat with 8th USAAF.
First 8th USAAF aircraft over Berlin 3/3/44.
Destroyed more enemy locomotives than any other group.
Site now industrial and agriculture.
How to get there: Turn west off Sudbury to Colchester Road at Wormingford,
signed Fordham, take first turn right, memorial on left O/S 168 929 309.

Plaques on Wormingford Memorial

Wormingford Memorial

Ashby
Suffolk

Memorial to the pilots of 2 P47 fighters which crashed in a nearby lake on 11th April 1945.
Both P47s were from 5th Emergency Rescue Sqn. from Halesworth. Suffolk.

The Memorial also Commemorates 5 Crew Members of a B17 from 100BG (H) Thorpe Abbots Norfolk which crashed on 11th May 1944.

Memorial outside Ashby Church.
O/S ref. 134 489990.

Aston Clinton
Buckinghamshire

Brass plaque in church to crew of B24 Bomber from 406 Night Leaflet squadron Cheddington which crashed locally 3rd January 1945.
How to get there: In Aston Clinton Village Church south of A41 road.
O/S ref. 165 879 119.

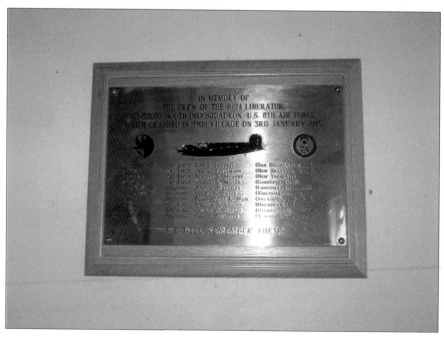

Plaque in Aston Clinton Church

Barsham
Suffolk

Memorial plaque to crew of B24 Bomber from 467 BG (H) Rackheath which
crashed nearby 22nd April 1944.
How to get there: Memorial is on north side of A143 at Barsham between Bungay
and Beccles. O/S ref. 156 396 895.

Plaque on Barsham Memorial

Carleton Rode Church
Norfolk

Memorial plaque to the crews of two B24 Bombers from 389 BG (H) from Hethel
which crashed after a collision over this village 21st November 1944.
Also plaque to the crew of a B24 Bomber from 463 BG (H) Old Buckenham
which crashed 9th February 1945.
How to get there: Plaques in Carleton Rode Village Church east of Old
Buckenham Airfield. O/S ref.144 115 925.

Cawston
Norfolk

Memorial to 2 crew members of a B17 Bomber (Lucky Strike) from
381 BG.(H) based at Ridgewell Suffolk which crashed at Cawston on
4th January 1944 whilst returning from a mission over Germany.

Memorial near Church at Cawston

Cheshunt
Hertfordshire

Memorial plaque to crew of B24 Bomber from 398 BG(H) Wendling which crashed nearby 12th August 1944.

How to get there: Plaque in the Central Library Cheshunt also duplicate plaque at Madinglay US War Cemetery. O/S ref. 166 358 021.

Cheshunt Memorial

Greenstead Green Church
Essex

Plaque to 2nd. Lt. Dwight G. Belt, pilot of a P47 from 78th. Fighter Group from Duxford which crashed behind this church 1st October 1944.
How to get there: Turn south off A1124 between Halstead and Earls Colne, signed for Greenstead Green, church is on right.
O/S ref. 168 821 285.

Plaque in Greenstead Green Church

Hardwick
Norfolk

Memorial Cross to B24 crew which crashed on take off at end of runway on 19th
December 1944.
Cross in field on sharp bend in road at south end of runway.
O/S ref. 134 255901.

Harling Farm
East Harling Norfolk

Plaque on piggery at Harling Farm, which replaces the building destroyed in
January 1945 when a Liberator C109 Tanker crashed on it killing the crew.
The tanker was taking off from Snetterton Heath Airfield but I have been unable
to trace the unit it was from.

Plaque on Piggery at Harling Farm

Hemel Hempstead
Hertfordshire

Gade Tower, Apsley, Hemel Hempstead.
Memorial Plaque to Lt. C.D.Blake who served with 406 NL Sqn.
At Cheddington Bucks. Killed whilst bailing out from a B24 which was struck by
lightning over Hemel Hempstead on 20th January 1945.
O/S ref. 166 061047.

Plaque on wall outside Gade Tower

Kirby Bedon
Norfolk

Memorial plaque in Kirby Bedon Church to four members of the crew of a B24 Bomber from 467th BG(H) Rackheath which crashed nearby on 18th of August 1944.
O/S ref.134 279054.

Norwich
Norfolk

Memorial plaque on block of flats in Heigham Street Norwich, in memory of the crew of a B24 Bomber from 458th BG, serving at
Horsham St. Faiths Norfolk, which Crashed in Baker Street opposite the site of this plaque.
O/S 134 221097.

Penn
Buckinghamshire

Roll of Honor of Crew of B17 Bomber (Tomahawk Warrior) from 398 BG (H) Nuthamstead which crashed locally on 12th August 1944. Their names are included in a beautifully bound book "Men of Penn" recording the names of local men killed in the second world war.

How to get there: In Penn Village Church beside B474 road.

O/S ref. 175 917 932.

Page 1 Memorial in " Men of Penn "

Page 2 of Roll of Honor in " Men of Penn "

Princes Riseborough
Buckinghamshire

Memorial plaque to 2nd Lt. Clyde Sparky Cosper of 367 Sqn. 306 BG(H) from Thurleigh, who was killed in B17 Bomber crash near this village on 13th October 1943.
Memorial is in centre of Princes Riseborough outside library.
O/S ref. 165 809 033.

Reedham
Norfolk

Memorial in Reedham Village to the crews of 2 B17 Bombers which collided over Hall
Farm, Reedham Marshes on 21st February 1944.
Both B17s were from 385 BG (H) Ridgewell, one from 549 Sqn the other from 550 Sqn
who were on their last mission to complete their tour of duty.
Memorial O/S 134 418016.

Memorial in Reedham Village

Thorpe Abbotts
Norfolk

Memorial to General Curtis E. Lemay Commander of The Third Air
Division 8th USAAF.
How to get there: Memorial is near car park in Thorpe Abbotts 100 BG(H) Museum.
O/S ref.156 188 813

Upper Sheringham
Norfolk

Memorial in churchyard at Upper Sheringham to the crew of B24 Bomber
(Alfred) from 392nd BG(H) at Wendling which crashed nearby on
4th January 1944.
O/s ref. 133 144419.

> Norwich - B24 cwh

> 2 AD   Memial

> Kettringhm   Holl

Walcott   Hall   67 FW

66 FW

65 FW

100ing3

2 AD.w

3 ADms

NORFOLK (20)
Suffolk. (18)